I'VE NEVER SEEN A WORM LIKE YOU
published by Gold 'n' Honey Books
a division of Multnomah Publishers, Inc.

© 1998 by Ray Butrum

Illustrations © 1998 by Jim Chapman

Design by Randy Robinson

International Standard Book Number: 1-57673-311-4

Printed in China

For information:
MULTNOMAH PUBLISHERS, INC.
POST OFFICE BOX 1720
SISTERS, OREGON 97759

98 99 00 01 02 03 04 — 10 9 8 7 6 5 4 3 2 1

I've Never Seen a Worm Like You

By Ray Butrum
Illustrated by Jim Chapman

Gold'n'Honey Books

I'm glad I get to go to school, but I love this time of year
When I can stay at home and play because spring break is here.
My backyard is amazing; it's an explorer's dream,
With giant rocks and many trees, all bordered by a stream.

6

I climbed into the big oak tree and found a fuzzy worm.
I touched it with my finger and we both began to squirm!

9

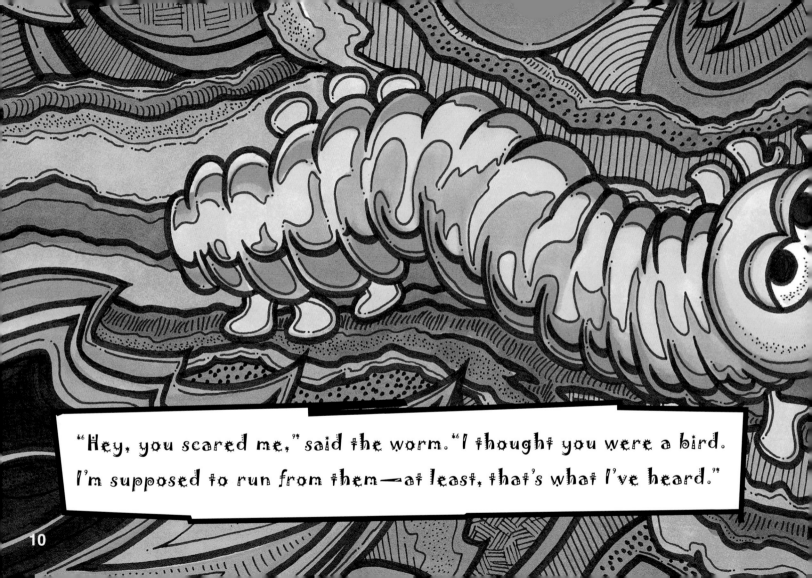

"Hey, you scared me," said the worm. "I thought you were a bird. I'm supposed to run from them—at least, that's what I've heard."

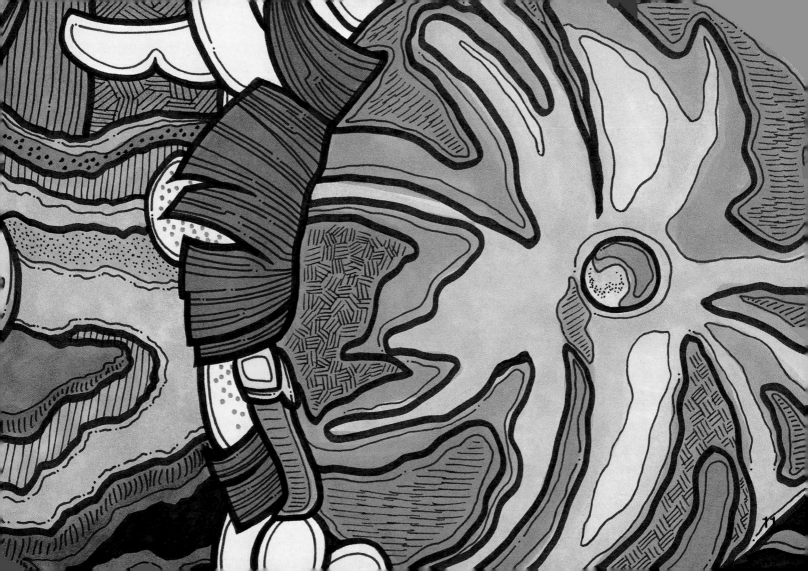

"Yes, you should," I told the worm, "or otherwise you'd be
A lunch or dinner for that bird and for her family.

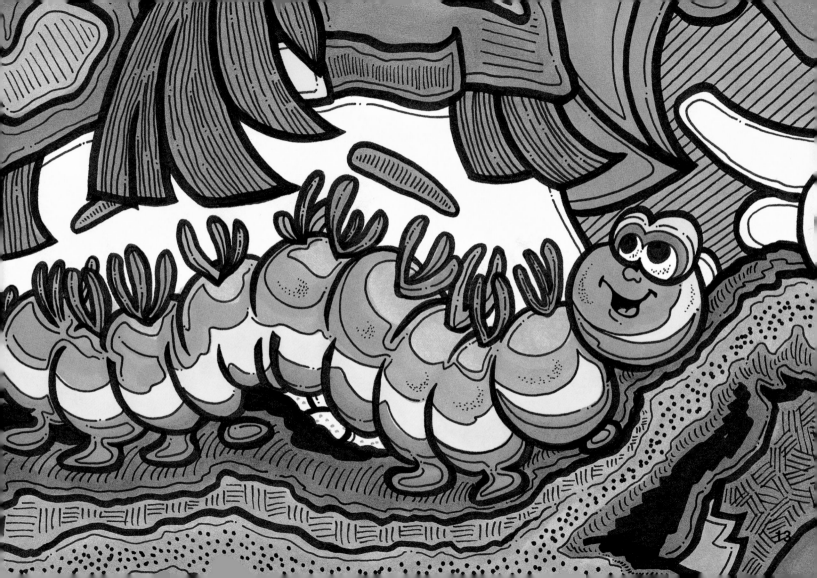

14

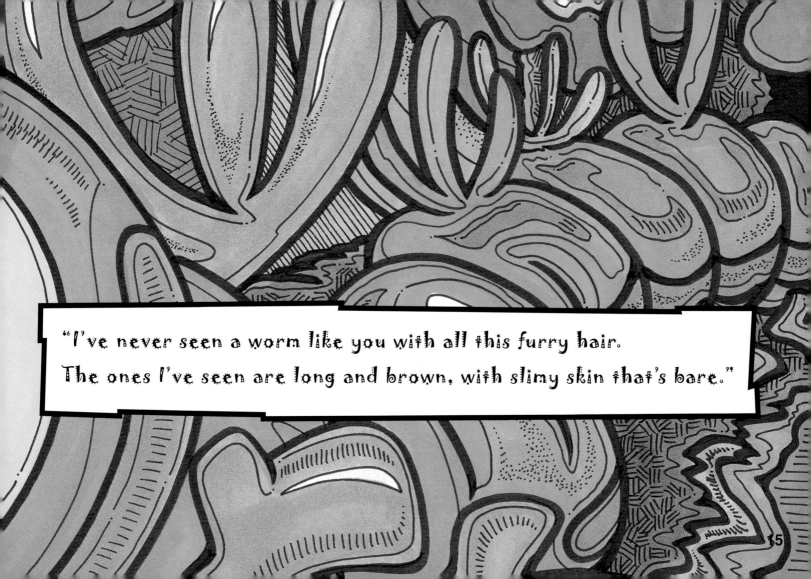

"I've never seen a worm like you with all this furry hair.
The ones I've seen are long and brown, with slimy skin that's bare."

"Well, I'm a caterpillar. I won't always look like this.
I'm going through a major change called metamorphosis.
First I hatched from a tiny egg; I'm a larva at this stage.
Next I'll form a chrysalis that's like a tiny cage.

"Built into the chrysalis is a nature-changing feature.
And when at last I leave it, I'll be a whole new creature."

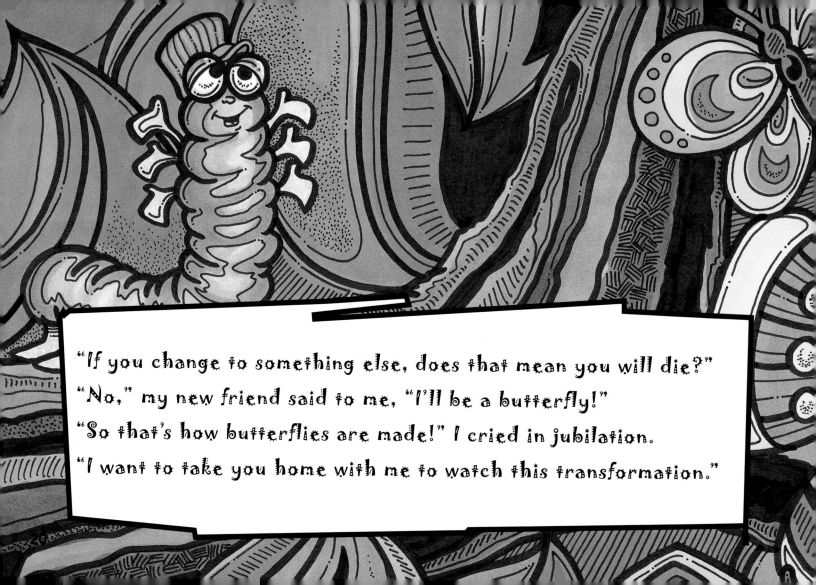

"If you change to something else, does that mean you will die?"

"No," my new friend said to me, "I'll be a butterfly!"

"So that's how butterflies are made!" I cried in jubilation.

"I want to take you home with me to watch this transformation."

I made a room for my new pet, complete with branch and box. And just to keep him comfy, I made his bed from socks.

22

23

Just as he had promised, a chrysalis did appear.
I had to practice patience as the final change drew near.

Each morning I would check to see if the cycle was complete.
Had he grown some pretty wings, antennae, and six feet?
When I saw a tear in the chrysalis, I let out a shout.
My wait was finally over—my friend was coming out!

He slowly spread his fragile wings so they could flutter dry.
And that is how you start your life if you're a butterfly.

Glossary

A **BUTTERFLY** is an insect with large, colorful wings, a slender body, and antennae.

A **CATERPILLAR** is the fuzzy wormlike larva of a butterfly.

A **CHRYSALIS** is the case a caterpillar weaves to enclose itself as it changes into a butterfly.

The **LARVA** of an animal is the early form it takes before metamorphosis.

METAMORPHOSIS means changing from one form to another.

A **STREAM** is water that flows in a small, natural channel.

A **TRANSFORMATION** is when something changes from one form to another.

A **WORM** is a small, long, soft-bodied animal that tunnels in the ground.